Now you see me ...

... now you don't!

Now you do.
Or do you?!

Heill!
The Vikings were awesome warriors, sailors, navigators, craftspeople, farmers, traders and storytellers. But one thing they weren't good at was writing down their history – I imagine that they were too busy doing all those other things! What we know about the Vikings comes from the writings of travellers who met them; from archaeologists who study Viking artefacts, like ships, weapons and bones; and from their sagas – although even these were written down after the Viking age. I have so enjoyed learning about the Vikings and suspect that there is still more to find out about these brave and creative people. Maybe you will be the one to make the next great Viking discovery – be sure to let me know if you do!
Loki, that naughty, shape-shifting Viking god, has insisted on appearing in the margins of this book with some extra facts. Good luck recognising him as he can change into an animal, a fish, a bird, an insect, a puff of smoke or even a dragon! You can also find out more about the lives of Viking families at the bottom of each page.
Gothan dag – as the Vikings might have said.
Marcia

For Mads Nobeard and his four dragons

First published 2020 by Walker Books Ltd, 87 Vauxhall Walk, London SE11 5HJ

2 4 6 8 10 9 7 5 3 1

Text and illustrations © 2020 Marcia Williams

The right of Marcia Williams to be identified as author/illustrator of this work has been asserted by her in accordance with the Copyright, Designs and Patents Act 1988

This book has been typeset in Tryst

Printed in China

All rights reserved. No part of this book may be reproduced, transmitted or stored in an information retrieval system in any form or by any means, graphic, electronic or mechanical, including photocopying, taping and recording, without prior written permission from the publisher.

British Library Cataloguing in Publication Data: a catalogue record for this book is available from the British Library

ISBN 978-1-4063-9217-3

www.walker.co.uk

The VIKINGS
RAIDERS, TRADERS and ADVENTURERS

MARCIA WILLIAMS

WALKER BOOKS
AND SUBSIDIARIES
LONDON • BOSTON • SYDNEY • AUCKLAND

The Incredible Vikings

Viking storytellers were called skalds.

They memorised stories of Norse heroes, gods and goddesses.

The Vikings loved poetry; it was considered a sport.

Viking means "raiding" or "raider" and is used to describe people from Sweden, Denmark and Norway between about 790 and 1066. This was when the most adventurous Vikings set out in their ships to explore new lands. Many Vikings went as warriors and raiders, but others sailed off in search of new farmland, or to trade. It is easy to imagine that all Vikings were seafarers, but many stayed on shore. The Vikings were brilliant farmers, skilled craftspeople, remarkable boat-builders, great hunters and truly amazing poets and storytellers.

THE VIKINGS NOT ONLY BELIEVED THAT THEIR GODS HAD POWER OVER THEM,

Yggdrasil, The Tree Of Life

ASGARD — HOME TO THE AESIR GODS
VALHALLA — A GREAT HALL FOR THE HEROIC DEAD
YGGDRASIL
BIFROST — RAINBOW BRIDGE
ALFHEIM — HOME OF THE LIGHT ELVES, WHO ARE MORE BEAUTIFUL THAN THE SUN
MIDGARD — HOME TO HUMANS
MUSPELHEIM — HOME TO THE FIRE GIANTS
VANAHEIM — HOME OF THE VANIR GODS, A DIFFERENT TRIBE TO THE AESIR GODS
NIDAVELLIR — HOME OF THE DWARVES – SKILLED CRAFTSMEN AND FORGERS
JOTUNHEIM — HOME OF THE GIANTS
NIFLHEIM — A WORLD OF ICE, FOG AND MIST
HELHEIM — HOME OF THE GODDESS HEL AND THE DEAD

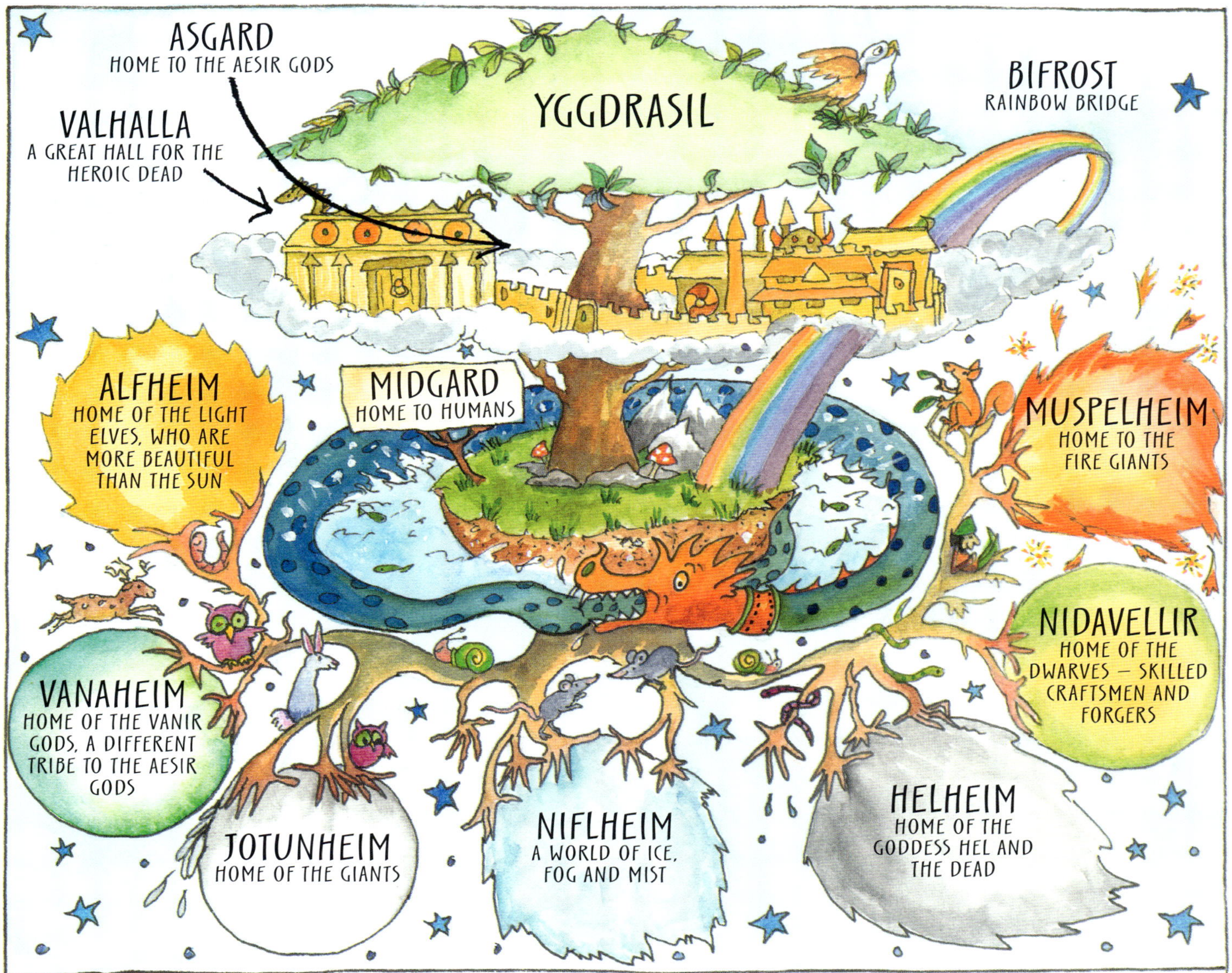

Viking stories were often about the gods, dwarves, giants and other mythical creatures that the Vikings believed lived alongside them. According to the Vikings, all beings lived in the nine worlds created by Odin, king of the gods, and his brothers, Ve and Vili. At the centre of these worlds was Yggdrasil, the tree of life. The finest of the nine worlds was Asgard, land of the gods. From Asgard a rainbow bridge stretched to Midgard, the home of the humans that was circled by Jormungand, the world serpent.

Viking warriors drew courage from their belief in an afterlife.

Those who died in battle were thought to be heroes.

They would join Odin in the great hall, Valhalla, on Asgard.

We'll remember our dead. Make sacrifices? Yes, to the gods and spirits. In return the gods will help us catch lots of fish... Oh. Harvest lots of veg... And sail safely. We must keep them happy!

BUT THAT SPIRITS, GIANTS, ELVES, DWARVES AND DRAGONS ALL MEDDLED IN HUMAN AFFAIRS.

The Viking Gods

I'm here and also in the picture – I'm a real trickster!

The Vikings love stories about me and other gods.

But especially about me and the gods' battles with the giants.

"My one-eyed hero!"

"Caw!"

"Weeds."

ODIN
KING OF THE GODS
He sacrificed an eye for greater wisdom and could see into the future. Hugin and Munin, Odin's two raven spies, flew across Midgard every morning and returned in time for breakfast to report the day's news to Odin. They also accompanied Odin into battle.

FRIGG
QUEEN OF THE GODS
Frigg was the goddess of wisdom. She was the wife of Odin and mother of Baldur. Like Odin, she could see into the future.

BALDUR
GOD OF LIGHT
Baldur was very handsome! He was loved and protected by all the gods, apart from Loki!

LOKI
TRICKSTER GOD
Clever and cunning, Loki was the son of a giant and loved to create mischief. He was unpopular with the rest of the gods and eventually caused the death of Baldur.

Odin was the most powerful of all the Viking gods. He was a fearsome war god, but also a god of poetry who was always ready to entertain his friends. From his throne, Hlidskjalf, he ruled over all the other Aesir gods. He had two ravens, two wolves, and an eight-legged horse that he rode into battle. His spear, Gungnir, was made by the dwarves that lived in Nidavellir. It never missed its target! Wise but unpredictable, Odin was worshipped by kings and chieftains.

"No wonder you fell, you're not wearing Thor's hammer."

"Why is our harvest so poor?"

"Dad frightened away the field spirits by bringing his ship's dragon head on land."

THE VIKINGS THOUGHT ALL DISASTERS WERE CAUSED BY ANGRY GODS OR EVIL SPIRITS.

TYR
GOD OF WAR AND JUSTICE
He lost a hand to the wolf, Fenrir.

"Ouch!"

THOR
GOD OF THUNDER
When he fought giants with his hammer, Mjöllnir, he created thunder and lightning. Two goats pulled his chariot.

NJORD
GOD OF THE WIND AND THE SEA
Viking fishermen and merchants prayed to him for calm waters before setting sail. He was the father of Freya and Freyr.

FREYA
GODDESS OF BEAUTY AND LOVE
When her husband, Odr, vanished, Freya wept tears of gold. She wore a magic cloak of falcon feathers.

FREYR
GOD OF FAIR WEATHER, HARVESTS AND WEALTH
He was Freya's brother and one of the most powerful and best-loved gods.

"Odin likes Baldur more than me."

"When Baldur steps on the ground, flowers grow."

"I call that over the top!"

From the fertile soil of Asgard, the goddess Frigg was born. She married Odin and they had a son, Baldur, the handsome god of light. Over time, many other gods were created. They often behaved like humans and argued with each other, but were still seen as powerful, and people prayed to each one for different reasons. The Vikings believed that the gods could bring them good fortune or bad, according to what they deserved or the value of their sacrifices!

"We'd better make a sacrifice to cheer them up."
"Should we sacrifice Dad?"
"Aah, he's not that bad!"
"I'll call on old Uncle Thorveld, he'll help us."

THEY WORE AMULETS FOR PROTECTION AND OFTEN CALLED ON THEIR ANCESTORS FOR HELP.

The Viking World

The Vikings had no compass.

They navigated by the stars, the sun and the moon ...

the movement of birds ...

The Vikings came from the part of northern Europe that we call Scandinavia. Before 790, most Vikings stayed close to home, fishing, farming, hunting and trading with each other. Scandinavia is an icy cold part of the world with long hours of darkness in the winter, so many nights would be spent by a fire, sharing stories and songs of battling gods, warriors and giants. Most Vikings couldn't read, so stories were passed on by word of mouth in a language called Old Norse.

IT TOOK MANY HOURS TO BUILD A LONGSHIP, MAKE THE ROPES AND WEAVE THE SAILS.

Encouraged by the heroic tales of their gods, the Vikings were brave and adventurous. They were also incredible boat-builders – so it isn't really surprising that they eventually put to sea. Most sailors in those days hugged the coastline for fear of getting lost in unknown waters. But the Vikings developed sails for their longships, which made it easier to travel long distances. Vikings were also excellent navigators, and over time they travelled as far as North America one way and the Middle East the other.

SHIP CARPENTERS WERE PAID WELL. THEIR SKILL WAS THE KEY TO VIKING SAFETY AND SUCCESS.

Going A'Viking!

There were many reasons why the Vikings started exploring and raiding other lands.

Some Viking raids only involved a few ships.

They needed more farmland and places to trade. Viking sagas also encouraged them to be war-like and adventurous.

One of the earliest recorded Viking raids was in 793, when a group of Vikings set off across the dangerous open seas.

Vikings relied on their superior weapons ...

and the element of surprise.

At Lindisfarne Priory, off the coast of northern England, people believed they saw ominous whirlwinds, comets and fire-breathing dragons in the skies. They were omens of the Viking attack that was approaching!

VIKING SOCIETY WAS SPLIT INTO THREE GROUPS: JARLS, KARLS AND THRALLS.

The Christian monks at the priory were unprepared for the terrible violence that struck them when the Vikings landed.

The warriors attacked without mercy. Some monks survived only to be drowned in the sea or taken as slaves.

The priory was ransacked and its treasure carried to the Viking ships. With their booty stowed and a new story to tell, the Vikings returned home for the winter – but come the spring they would be on the seas again!

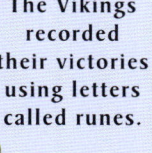

The Vikings recorded their victories using letters called runes.

They were carved onto stones or wood.

Sagas and poetry about all of their triumphs were learned by heart.

MOST VIKINGS DID NOT LIVE BEYOND THEIR FORTIES, SO CHILDREN TOOK ON ADULT TASKS.

Ragnar Shaggy Breeches

Ragnar was called Shaggy Breeches because of his fur trousers.

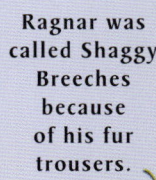

They were made by his favourite wife, Aslaug, who bore him four sons.

Viking kings and other powerful men were allowed more than one wife.

- IRON HELMET. OFTEN WITH A BAR TO PROTECT THE NOSE.
- WEALTHY WARRIORS HAD CHAINMAIL SHIRTS MADE OF IRON RINGS.
- BATTLE SCAR – OUCH!
- VIKINGS MAY HAVE HUNTED WITH BIRDS OF PREY.
- LIME WOOD SHIELD WITH METAL STUDS AND CENTRAL BOSS.
- AXE – SHARP AND LETHAL!
- DOUBLE-EDGED IRON SWORD.
- SHAGGY TROUSERS FROM A SHAGGY ANIMAL.
- GOATSKIN BOOTS.

After the successful raid on Lindisfarne, undefended monasteries and churches became favourite targets for Vikings such as the legendary warrior, Ragnar Lothbrok – also known as Shaggy Breeches! King of Denmark and Sweden in the ninth century, Ragnar was fearless in battle. He believed he was descended from the great god Odin and was therefore invincible!

- Surprise is our best weapon.
- And the speed of our ships!
- What about our skill as fighters?
- We are second to none.

VIKING RAIDERS CARRIED PLENTY OF FOOD, WATER AND WEAPONS ABOARD THEIR SHIPS.

In 845, Ragnar sailed south with 120 ships and 5,000 Vikings. He raided ports in England, Ireland and France, terrorising the people who lived there.

Ragnar liked to attack Christian cities on holy feast days when most of the guards would be in church.

When Ragnar sailed up the Seine estuary to Paris, the king gave him 7,000 livres of silver to stop looting the city!

Ragnar's end finally came in 865 when he invaded England and was defeated by Ælla, king of Northumbria. As revenge for the many deaths caused by Ragnar, King Ælla had him thrown into a pit of snakes. Their venom eventually overcame Ragnar, and robbed him of the glorious death on the battlefield that all Viking warriors longed for.

Some historians think Vikings decorated their bodies with tattoos.

Like many Viking stories, that might be more myth than history!

Maybe the stories about Ragnar are mostly myth!

IF THEY FOUND GOOD FARMING LAND THEY MIGHT RETURN LATER WITH THEIR FAMILIES.

15

Alfred the Great and Danelaw

Wessex was in the south of England.

The other main kingdoms were Northumbria, Mercia and East Anglia.

The Vikings continued to raid Britain, home to the Anglo-Saxons, but they were no longer only plundering riches – they now wanted to take land. At the time, England was divided into kingdoms and the Vikings conquered nearly all of them. In 871, when Alfred the Great became the ruler of Wessex, the last independent kingdom, he determined to keep them out.

But King Alfred was eventually known as "king of the English".

The Viking army roaming England was larger than any that had attacked before. Alfred tried to make peace, but the Vikings kept coming back. In spite of King Alfred's fierce defences, he lost several battles to the Vikings. Alfred refused to give up, and eventually he managed to defeat the army led by Guthrum, king of the Danes, at the Battle of Edington in 878.

THE "THING" WAS AN ASSEMBLY WHERE LAWS WERE MADE AND CRIMES WERE JUDGED.

King Alfred and Guthrum signed a peace treaty, and Guthrum agreed to be baptised a Christian, like most Anglo-Saxons.

Alfred gave the Vikings a large area of England and called it Danelaw. Guthrum ruled in the area of East Anglia until his death in 890.

The Vikings who settled in Danelaw were mostly farmers. They kept their own laws and spoke Old Norse, but gradually this merged with the Old English spoken by the Anglo-Saxons. Danelaw lasted for less than fifty years, but the influence of the Vikings on British language, culture and customs still remains today.

LAWS WERE PASSED ON BY WORD OF MOUTH. PEOPLE WHO BROKE THE LAW BECAME "OUTLAWS".

17

Ethelred and Danegeld

This was a terrible time for England.

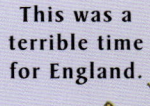

"Not ready for the Vikings!"

"Still not ready!"

"Definitely not ready!"

After Alfred the Great died, Anglo-Saxon kings started to take land back from Danelaw. But not all kings were strong enough to fight for their land. When ten-year-old Ethelred, known as the Unready or Ill-advised, became king in 978, he was no match for the Vikings.

The Vikings plundered many towns.

"You have to do something, your Majesty."
"Pay them to go away!"

Ethelred tried to stop a new wave of Viking raids by giving them gold, known as Danegeld.

"This means no more raids."
"Oh, of course ... until the next one!"

But the Vikings were not stupid. They took the Danegeld and continued their attacks!

Sweyn's sister was killed in the attack on Danelaw.

"This is not a good plan!"

In 1002, King Ethelred's soldiers killed thousands of Viking families living in Danelaw as revenge for the raids.

"We will destroy that Anglo-Saxon king and all his followers!"

When Sweyn Forkbeard, king of Denmark, learned of this atrocity, he was furious and determined to avenge his people!

AS WELL AS LEARNING TO MAN A BOAT AND NAVIGATE, VIKING WARRIORS LEARNED

18

Sweyn and his son invaded England with a vast fleet of longships full of fearless Viking warriors.

King Ethelred was no match for them and the Anglo-Saxons lost battle after battle.

Sweyn wanted to avenge his sister's death.

Ethelred fled to France, leaving his son, Edmund, to defend England.

Sweyn became king of England but died suddenly. His son Canute claimed the crown.

Canute was a fearless warrior.

More cruel and bloody battles were fought until finally Edmund and Canute agreed to a peace treaty. North of the River Thames would be ruled by Canute the Viking, while King Edmund would rule Wessex. At last there was peace in England.

Edmund was tougher than his father – just not tough enough!

SKILLS LIKE FARMING AND HUNTING SO THEY COULD PROVIDE FOR THEIR FAMILIES.

Canute the Great

Most Vikings turned to Christianity, but they never forgot their Norse gods.

Some Vikings continued to honour Odin and the other gods.

But Christian traders liked to trade with other Christians.

"Now you are king, Canute, perhaps you should spread Christianity among your people."

"Yes, then instead of raiding and destroying churches, I will rebuild them and give them money!"

Within weeks of signing the peace treaty, King Edmund suddenly died and in 1016 Canute was crowned king of all England. After journeying to Rome and meeting Pope John XIX, the head of the Catholic Church, Canute vowed to become a just ruler. He encouraged Christianity, reformed outdated laws and kept England free of Viking raids by paying a vast amount of money to get rid of any warriors still in the country. With peace from the Vikings, trade developed and England became richer. Towns grew up and many Vikings settled in England.

Can you teach me to weave as well as you? — If you teach me how to make finer needles. — I love your jewels. — My husband makes them. — I'll swap a necklace for some carrots. — That's so generous, dear friend. — Let's play together. — Yeah!

UNDER CANUTE'S RULE THE VIKINGS AND ANGLO-SAXONS LIVED IN HARMONY.

King Canute was greatly admired, but he hated false flattery. When a courtier declared that Canute could even command the sea, he had his throne carried to the beach.

As the tide turned and the sea crept towards his throne, Canute ordered it to stop. But the sea didn't listen to him and kept coming – proving Canute was not all powerful!

Canute married Ethelred's widow, Emma of Normandy.

In 1018 Canute's brother King Harald of Denmark died, so Canute claimed his throne.

Ten years later Canute invaded Norway and took the crown from King Olaf Haraldsson.

Maybe they married for love – or maybe it was political!

Canute called himself king of England, Denmark, Norway and some of Sweden – the greatest empire ever ruled by a Viking. As king of England, Canute was remarkable for being a Viking who gave generously to monasteries and churches, instead of raiding them! Even so, Canute always remained a Viking at heart and liked nothing better than listening to sagas.

Canute was the second English king to be called "great".

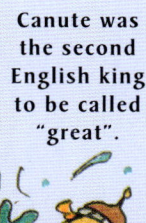

MANY VIKINGS TURNED FROM THEIR NORSE GODS AND BECAME CHRISTIANS.

Traders Not Raiders!

A Viking trading vessel is called a knarr.

Knarrs were smaller and deeper than longships.

Some Vikings traded in slaves captured on raids.

Not all Vikings spent their time going on raids. Some were traders who set sail in special merchant ships that could travel at sea, up rivers and be carried across land.

The Viking homelands were rich in timber, iron, furs, whale bone and walrus ivory. Some merchants traded these at home, but others looked for foreign markets where they could be exchanged for goods not found locally.

Merchants wanted safe places to trade so market towns were built, both in Viking lands and abroad. Merchants paid taxes to local rulers in return for the right to trade in peace.

VIKING WOMEN RAN HOUSEHOLDS AND FARMS WHILE THE MEN WERE AWAY ON EXPEDITIONS.

In about 862, a Viking called Rurik crossed the Baltic Sea and then travelled up-river to the village of Novgorod, in modern-day Russia.

He built defences to protect the village from raiders, organised a market and was soon ruling over a thriving community.

Before the Vikings had coins they exchanged goods.

Later Oleg, another Viking and a possible relative of Rurik, settled further south in Kiev, in modern-day Ukraine. He turned it into another successful centre for trade.

Or they paid with hack silver, made from cut-up jewellery or foreign coins.

Not even the freezing winters in Russia stopped the traders: they just travelled along the frozen rivers in boat-sleighs instead of ships. Gradually, the Vikings built up a network of markets, meaning they could trade greater distances, eventually reaching Jerusalem and Constantinople, capital of the Byzantine Empire. This made the Vikings rich and powerful!

The first Danish coins appeared in the ninth century.

A WOMAN COULD CHOOSE HER HUSBAND AND DIVORCE HIM IF HE TREATED HER BADLY.

When Erik returned to Iceland he encouraged others to move to his newly found land. In 985 he led an expedition of twenty-five ships to the country he called Greenland. There were many storms on the way – some ships were wrecked and others forced back to Iceland.

Eventually, fourteen ships reached the west coast of Greenland where the Vikings founded two settlements. Although there was some good farmland and the seas were rich with life, there were few trees for boats, buildings or fuel, and most of the island was permanently covered in snow. Even so, many generations of Vikings managed to forge a living there. But Erik the Red's son, Leif Erikson, decided to leave in search of a new land.

Erik named the country Greenland because it sounded more tempting than Freezingland!

The settlers took horses, cows, sheep and oxen with them.

But they relied on hunting and fishing to survive.

THEY SANK THE HOUSES INTO THE GROUND TO PROTECT THEM FROM THE COLD.

Leif Erikson Reaches North America

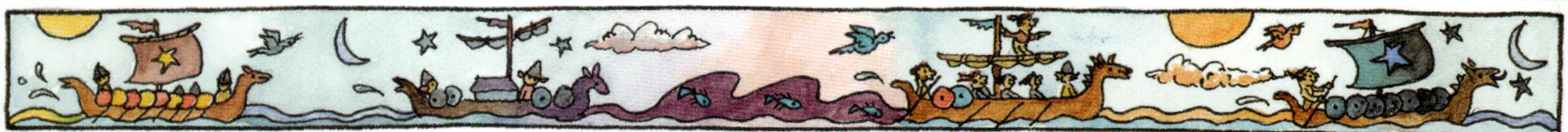

Leif named his discovery Vinland because wild grapes grew there.

He is thought to have landed in modern-day Newfoundland, in Canada.

Leif was the first European to set foot there.

Trees, berries, warm sun and calm seas. We must be in Valhalla!

Seems deserted, apart from the wildlife.

In about 1000, Leif Erikson sailed west to look for a land that a Viking trader had seen from afar. Leif and his crew soon reached land, but it was cold and bleak, so they sailed further south until he spied lush-looking land suitable for farming. Excitedly, Leif and his men beached their boat and went ashore. There appeared to be no one else there, but there was plenty to hunt and fish and lots of wood, so they built a camp and spent the winter there. Leif named the land Vinland.

BEFORE A SEA VOYAGE THE VIKINGS WOULD CHECK FOR CALM AND CLEAR WEATHER.

The following spring, Leif returned to Greenland with news of his discovery. His brother, Thorvald, decided to lead an expedition to Vinland. Thorvald and his men arrived and started to explore, but discovered that there were Native Americans already living in Vinland. After one unfriendly encounter Thorvald was killed, and afterwards the rest of his men went back to Greenland. Another expedition was attempted later, but in the end the Vikings decided that North America was not the place for them.

"Thorvald, look out!"

The Native Americans outnumbered the Vikings ...

and fought to defend their land.

The Vikings called the Native Americans "Skraelings".

EVEN SO, MANY SHIPS WERE WRECKED OR BLOWN OFF COURSE AND NEVER HEARD OF AGAIN.

The Last Great Viking

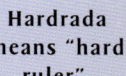
Hardrada means "hard ruler".

"Dear neighbour, can I help you?" "Really?" "Kill you, friend? Never!" "Really?"

By 1066 the Vikings had given up their war-like ways and lived or traded peacefully in places they had once raided, including England.

"I've been fighting since I was fifteen, I'm not going to give up now!"

All except for the king of Norway, Harald Sigurdsson, nicknamed Hardrada. He remained an ambitious warmonger.

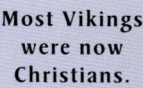
Most Vikings were now Christians.

"Surprise, another Viking attack." "I'm not giving up my crown to you, Hardrada!"

Hardrada attacked England from the north, believing he had a claim to King Harold II's crown. He captured York, and King Harold had to gather an army to face him.

I think it all went wrong for the Vikings when they stopped worshipping me...

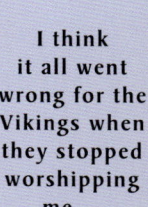

"You won't have my crown you Viking knave!" "Oh yes I will!"

King Harold reached the north so quickly it took Hardrada by surprise.

"Let's hope this is the end of those pesky Vikings!"

Eventually Hardrada was killed in a huge battle and King Harold kept his crown.

"Tell us about Thor, Dad." "No, Odin." "I like Loki and the giants." "What about Freya or Frigg?" "How about I have a snooze!"

EVEN CHRISTIAN VIKINGS LOVED TO HEAR STORIES ABOUT THE ANCIENT NORSE GODS.

 and the other Norse gods.

 But mostly me, Loki the trickster god!

Just three days later, William, Duke of Normandy landed close to Hastings in the south of England. He also believed he had a claim to the English throne. Exhausted by their battles with Hardrada and their long journey back, and heavily outnumbered, Harold's men struggled to repel William's forces. On 14th October 1066, King Harold was killed at the Battle of Hastings and William became king of England. William was a descendant of a Viking called Rollo, so it could be said that the Vikings finally succeeded in vanquishing the Anglo-Saxons! This is seen as the end of the Viking age, but there is no doubt that those raiding, trading, Viking adventurers had a lasting impact on language, art, technology and culture all over the world!

 I just don't get enough attention these days!

JUST AS THEY LOVED TO SHARE TALES OF THEIR VIKING ANCESTORS' AMAZING ADVENTURES!

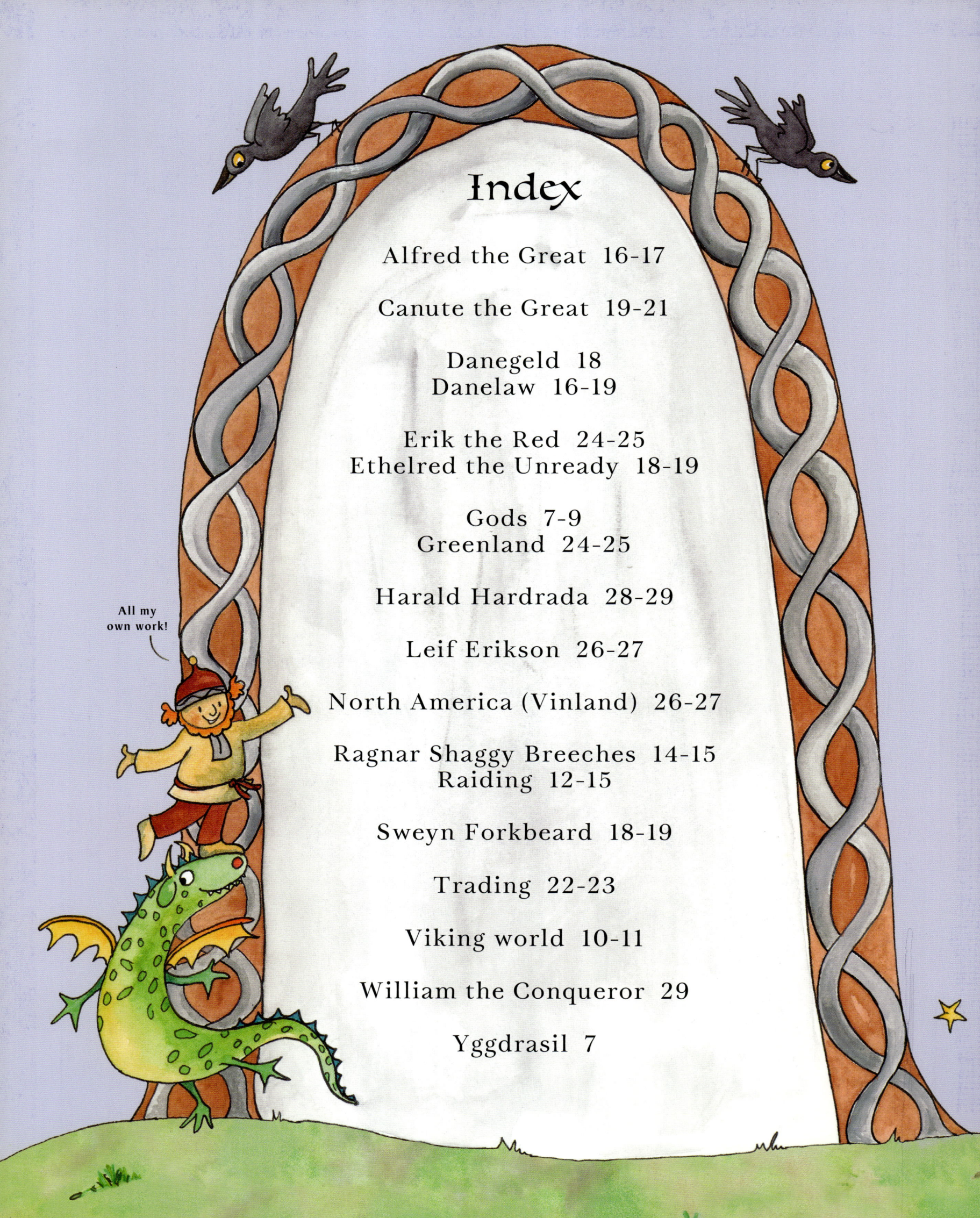